from SEA TO SHINING SEA

GEORGIA

By Dennis Brindell Fradin

CONSULTANTS

N. Nannette McGee, Consultant, Social Studies Education, Georgia Department of Education

Anne P. Smith, Director, Georgia Historical Society

Robert L. Hillerich, Ph.D., Consultant, Pinellas County Schools, Florida;
Visiting Professor, University of South Florida

CHILDREN'S PRESS
A Division of Grolier Publishing
Sherman Turnpike
Danbury, Connecticut 06816

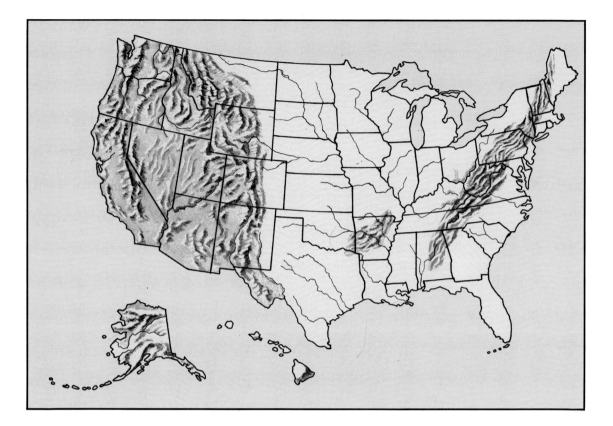

Georgia is the largest of the fourteen states in the region called the South. The other southern states are Alabama, Arkansas, Delaware, Florida, Kentucky, Louisiana, Maryland, Mississippi, North Carolina, South Carolina, Tennessee, Virginia, and West Virginia.

For Judy, a great wife and researcher

Front cover picture: A twilight view of Atlanta; page 1: dunes on St. Simons Island; back cover: Providence Canyon State Park

Project Editor: Joan Downing
Design Director: Karen Kohn
Research Assistant: Judith Bloom Fradin
Typesetting: Graphic Connections, Inc.
Engraving: Liberty Photoengraving

9 10 11 12 13 14 R 02 01 00 99

Library of Congress Cataloging-in-Publication Data

Fradin, Dennis B.
  From sea to shining sea. Georgia / by Dennis Brindell Fradin.
    p. cm.
  Includes index.
  Summary: An overview of the Empire State of the South, introducing its history, geography, industries, sites of interest, and famous people.
  ISBN 0-516-03810-9
  1. Georgia—Juvenile literature. [1. Georgia.] I. Title.
F286.3.F65   1991   91-12101
975.8—dc20   CIP
                                              AC

Bluegrass musicians

Table of Contents

Introducing the Empire State of the South 4

Mountains, Woods, and Red Clay Hills 7

From Ancient Times Until Today 13

Georgians and Their Work 29

A Trip Through Georgia 33

A Gallery of Famous Georgians 47

Did You Know? 54

Georgia Information 56

Georgia History 58

Map of Georgia 60

Glossary 61

Index 63

Introducing the Empire State of the South

Georgia lies along the Atlantic Ocean in the southeastern United States. Blue ocean waters wash the coast and the Golden Isles. Red clay hills and green pine forests color the land. The Blue Ridge Mountains tower above northern Georgia. The state's warm southern climate also helps make it beautiful. Each year, Georgia is bright with budding trees and blooming flowers when much of America is still under snow.

Georgia is an important farming state, as two of its nicknames show. It is called the "Peach State," thanks to all the peaches grown by its farmers. It is called the "Goober State" because of all the peanuts (nicknamed "goobers") grown there. But today, industry means more than farming to Georgia. That is why Georgia today is also known as the "Empire State of the South."

Georgia has many other claims to fame. Where were civil-rights leader Dr. Martin Luther King, Jr., and President Jimmy Carter born? Where was an anesthetic first used in surgery? Where do the Braves play baseball and the Hawks play basketball? As you will see, the answer to these questions is: Georgia!

Overleaf: Providence
Canyon State Park

A picture map
of Georgia

DUNNINGTON

Mountains, Woods, and

Red Clay Hills

Mountains, Woods, and Red Clay Hills

Georgia ranks twenty-first in size among the fifty states. That makes it a little bigger than average. Yet Georgia's size is special in two ways. It is the largest of the twenty-six states that are east of the Mississippi River. And it is the largest of the fourteen states in the region called the South.

Five other southern states border Georgia. Tennessee and North Carolina are to the north. Florida is to the south. Alabama is Georgia's main western neighbor. South Carolina and the Atlantic Ocean are to the east. Georgia has hundreds of off-shore islands. Eight of them—Ossabaw, Wassaw, St.

St. Simons Island is a popular vacation spot.

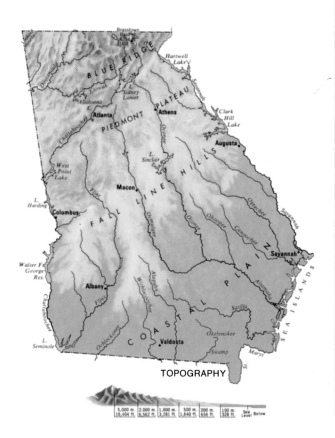

Catherines, St. Simons, Jekyll, Sea, Sapelo, and Cumberland—are known as the Golden Isles.

Anna Ruby Falls, in Unicoi State Park

TOPOGRAPHY

Georgia generally slopes downhill from its far northern highlands to the sea in the southeast. The Appalachian and Blue Ridge mountains run through northern Georgia. The state's highest peak is in the Blue Ridge Mountains. Its name is Brasstown Bald Mountain. It rises 4,784 feet above sea level.

Okefenokee Swamp

A hilly region of the country called the Piedmont runs through Georgia south of the mountains. Piedmont means "foot of the mountain." The Piedmont lies between Georgia's far northern mountains and its flat southern plains. The Georgia Piedmont is known for its red hills. Their color comes from red clay. The Piedmont is also Georgia's most-populated area. Three of Georgia's four largest cities—Atlanta, Columbus, and Macon—are in the Piedmont.

Flatlands make up the southern half of Georgia. They are called the coastal plains. Many swamps and marshes can be found in the plains near the ocean.

Among them is Okefenokee Swamp, one of the nation's best-known wetlands.

Maps of Georgia often look as if they have many blue veins. That is because of all the state's rivers. Georgia's main rivers include the Savannah, the Ogeechee, the Oconee, the Ocmulgee, the Altamaha, the Flint, and the Chattahoochee. Most of the rivers flow downhill toward the southeast. Then they empty into the ocean.

Georgia is also one of the most-wooded states. Its main kinds of trees include pines, oaks, hickories, and cypresses. The state is so famous for its tall pines that people sometimes say "as tall as a Georgia pine" when they mean that something is very tall.

Overleaf: An 1899 photo of the main street of Flowery Branch on "Cotton Day"

Pines (left and middle) and cypresses (right) are among the main kinds of trees that are native to Georgia.

From Ancient Times

Until Today

FROM ANCIENT TIMES UNTIL TODAY

Millions of years ago, inland seas covered the southern half of Georgia. Sharks' teeth have been found 100 miles from what is now the ocean. Mammoths also lived in Georgia very long ago. They were much like modern elephants.

Ancient Indians reached Georgia at least ten thousand years ago. Many of Georgia's prehistoric Indians built mounds, or hills, of dirt and rock. Some mounds were burial places. Skeletons have been found inside. Other mounds supported buildings such as temples. Still others, including Rock Eagle Mound, look like huge animals.

CREEKS AND CHEROKEES

Two main groups of American Indians lived in Georgia in later times: the Creeks and the Cherokees. Another group was the Yamacraws.

As a people, the Indians were friendly and generous. They welcomed the first European settlers. But as time passed, the settlers returned this kindness with cruelty.

Prehistoric Indians who built mounds lived in many parts of what are now the eastern and central United States. This is the largest of the Etowah Indian Mounds.

Explorers and Early Settlers

Spanish explorer Hernando De Soto was the first known European in what is now Georgia. Between 1539 and 1542, De Soto explored much of the Southeast while looking for gold. His route took him through Georgia in 1540.

Spain began settling Florida in 1565. The Spaniards also hoped to rule Georgia. They named the area Guale. In 1566, the Spanish built a fort on St. Catherines Island. Soon after, Spanish priests built some missions in Guale. But Spain did little to settle the area.

England's Thirteenth Colony

England was the main nation to colonize America. By 1670, England ruled twelve American colonies. There were only two regions along the East Coast that England didn't rule. One was Spanish Florida. The other was Guale. By about 1690, the Spanish had left Guale. The region lay between England's twelve American colonies and Spanish Florida.

England wanted this land. About 1729, Englishman James Oglethorpe had an idea. At the time, debtors in England were often jailed.

Hernando De Soto did not find the gold he was seeking in south-eastern America.

James Oglethorpe (right) and the first Georgia settlers landed at Yamacraw Bluff in February 1733.

Oglethorpe thought debtors should be allowed to start a new life in Guale. He and his friends asked King George II to grant them the land between South Carolina and Florida.

In 1732, the king signed a paper creating Georgia. It was the last of England's thirteen American colonies. Twenty-one trustees would run Georgia's government. Among them was James Oglethorpe. He would also be Georgia's first governor.

It was soon decided that Georgia would not be just a colony for debtors. Other people would be allowed to move there, too. And, unlike the other colonies, Georgia was to have no slavery.

In November 1732, Governor Oglethorpe and about 120 settlers left England on a ship called the *Anne*. The *Anne* reached America in early 1733. Oglethorpe chose Yamacraw Bluff, along the Savannah River, for the site of Georgia's first town.

The small Yamacraw Indian tribe already lived there. The kindly Yamacraw chief, Tomochichi, said there was room for the settlers on the bluff.

Oglethorpe led the settlers to the bluff on February 12, 1733. They called their first town Savannah.

Life in Georgia was harder than the settlers had expected. They weren't used to the hot summers. That first summer, about forty colonists died of illness. Among them was the colony's doctor.

In July 1733, some Jewish people sailed into Savannah. One of them, Dr. Samuel Nunes, soon cured many of the sick Georgians. Ever since 1733, Savannah has had a good-sized Jewish population. In 1734, German-speaking Protestants called Salzburgers arrived. They founded Ebenezer, a town not far from Savannah. In 1735, Oglethorpe founded Augusta. In 1736, people from Scotland built Darien.

From 1739 to 1744, England and Spain fought a war over lands in the Americas. It was called the "War of Jenkins' Ear." On July 7, 1742, Governor Oglethorpe's army defeated the Spanish. The fight took place on St. Simons Island. This clash is called the Battle of Bloody Marsh because it was said that the ground turned red with Spanish blood. The

Tomochichi, the Yamacraw chief, with his adopted son

The War of Jenkins' Ear began after the Spanish reportedly cut off the ear of English ship captain Robert Jenkins.

17

English victory at Bloody Marsh meant that England would keep Georgia.

Meanwhile, Georgia was growing very slowly. Many colonists stayed away from Georgia because of its ban on slavery.

James Oglethorpe, who hated slavery, left Georgia forever in 1743. White Georgians wanted the trustees to allow slavery. When the trustees did this in 1750, thousands of new settlers came to Georgia. Many colonists bought one or two slaves to help with their farm work. Some families bought many slaves and built huge plantations. The slaves grew rice and other crops on the plantations.

By the early 1750s, the trustees gave Georgia up, and it became a royal colony. This meant that the king ruled it through his governors.

THE REVOLUTIONARY WAR

England was deeply in debt by 1763. English law-makers felt that Americans should help pay this debt. They began taxing the Americans.

Most Americans hated these taxes. They refused to pay the tax money. The arguing between America and England turned into war. We call it the Revolutionary War (1775-1783). The Americans

Before 1733, these areas along the Georgia coast had been settled.

18

fought it to turn the thirteen colonies into a new nation, the United States of America. In 1776, American leaders issued the Declaration of Independence. This paper explained why the United States was freeing itself from England. Georgia's three signers were Button Gwinnett, Lyman Hall, and George Walton.

At first, Georgia had no major Revolutionary War fighting. Then, in December 1778, the British captured Savannah. By the spring of 1780, England had seized all of Georgia but a small part near Augusta.

In the fall of 1781, the Americans won the Battle of Yorktown in Virginia. It was the key battle of the war. Their victory at Yorktown meant that the Americans would win the Revolution. General "Mad" Anthony Wayne was sent to help win back Georgia. In June 1782, General Wayne defeated several hundred Indians who were fighting for England. This was Georgia's last Revolutionary War battle. The British left Georgia the next month. In 1783, the war ended. America was free of England.

Costumed guides at Fort Frederica National Monument

In 1787, American leaders created the United States Constitution. It set up a framework of government for the new nation. William Few and

Abraham Baldwin signed the Constitution for Georgia. Each state would officially join the country when it approved the Constitution. Georgia became the fourth state on January 2, 1788.

KING COTTON

Soon after Georgia became a state, a young man named Eli Whitney moved there. A friend told Whitney that someone should invent a machine for cleaning seeds from cotton. At the time, cotton had to be cleaned by hand. By the spring of 1793, Whitney had created the cotton gin. It could clean cotton fifty times as fast as a person cleaning it by hand.

Eli Whitney (left) invented the cotton gin (right) in 1793.

Cotton began earning so much money that it became known as "King Cotton." Tens of thousands of families moved to Georgia to plant cotton. Tens of thousands of slaves were brought in to help with the work. By the 1820s, Georgia had become the world's leading cotton grower.

THE TRAIL OF TEARS

In the 1700s, most of Georgia's settlers had lived in the far eastern part of the state. But many people who moved there in the 1800s settled in central and western Georgia. They built new towns. Macon, in the heart of Georgia, was laid out in 1823. Columbus, in far western Georgia, was founded in 1827. Atlanta was founded in northwest Georgia in 1837. It was first called Terminus, because it was at the end of the Western and Atlantic Railroad line. A few years later, it was renamed Marthasville. Not until 1845 was the city named Atlanta.

Terminus means "end of the line."

As they moved westward, the settlers took more and more of the Indians' lands. The Creeks fought back. However, they were beaten by the Americans in the Creek War of 1813-14. By the late 1820s, the remaining Creeks had been pushed out of Georgia. Most of them were forced to settle in Oklahoma.

Sequoya (left) invented a Cherokee alphabet that was used to print newspapers and books.

Meanwhile, the Cherokees had a capital city called New Echota in northwest Georgia. They had their own schools. In 1821, a Cherokee named Sequoya worked out a writing system for his people. It was used to print a famous Indian newspaper, the *Cherokee Phoenix*. The Cherokees hoped they would always have a home in Georgia. Then, in 1827, gold was found in northern Georgia. Soon, Georgia was the scene of one of the nation's first gold rushes. And in the late 1830s, the Cherokees were forced to move to Oklahoma. Thousands of Cherokees died on the way to Oklahoma. The survivors called the route *Nunna-da-ul-tsun-yi*—the Trail of Tears.

THE CIVIL WAR

By the mid-1800s, southerners were arguing with northerners. The main topic was slavery. Many northerners felt that slavery was wrong. Southerners feared that the United States government would soon try to end slavery in the South, too. In 1860 and 1861, eleven southern states, including Georgia, left the United States. They formed the Confederate States of America, or the Confederacy.

The United States government said that the South couldn't leave the Union. War between the Union (the North) and the Confederacy (the South) began in 1861. It is called the Civil War (1861-1865). The Confederates won two great victories in northwest Georgia. They were the battles of Chickamauga Creek and Kennesaw Mountain.

The Confederates won a great victory at the Battle of Chickamauga Creek.

The Confederacy did not have enough troops and supplies to win the war, though. As the end neared for the Confederacy, Georgia took a terrible beating. In the summer of 1864, Union forces under General William Tecumseh Sherman captured Atlanta. They burned most of the city. Sherman and his men then made their famous march to the sea. On the way, they burned plantations and farms. They ripped up railroad tracks and wrecked factories. Sherman captured Savannah in December 1864.

The Confederacy lost the Civil War in April 1865. About twenty-five thousand Georgians had died in the war. Much of Georgia looked as if it had been struck by a tornado.

THE MODERN STATE

Earlier Georgia capitals were Savannah (1733-1786), Augusta (1786-1795), Louisville (1796-1806), and Milledgeville (1807-1868).

Georgia was rebuilt after the Civil War. In 1868, Atlanta became Georgia's capital. In 1870, Georgia once again became part of the United States.

Georgians had to change their way of life. Slavery was ended in America in 1865. Without slave labor, cotton growing made less money. Later, in the 1920s, beetles called boll weevils wrecked much of the cotton crop. Georgians then started to grow peaches and peanuts.

Even more important was the growth of manufacturing (making products). Many factories were built in Georgia in the late 1800s and early 1900s. By 1950, more Georgians worked in factories than on farms. By the late 1980s, only about one of every thirty-five Georgia workers still farmed.

Georgians' ways of thinking had to change, too. Most white Georgians didn't feel that the freed slaves were their equals. They built a system in which Georgia had separate schools for black children. Neither black schools nor white schools were very good. As of 1935, Georgia had one of the nation's worst school systems. At that time, Georgia had no black lawmakers. This was true even though more than a third of its people were black. White Georgians also kept blacks from voting.

To make things worse, a hate group called the Ku Klux Klan (KKK) has been active in Georgia at times since the Civil War. KKK members and other white people have beaten up blacks. They even lynched (hanged) some of them in past times.

Several black Georgians led the fight for racial justice in America. The most famous of them was Dr. Martin Luther King, Jr. King was a great civil-rights leader of the 1950s and 1960s. He and other civil-rights workers reached some of their goals.

Dr. Martin Luther King, Jr., was born in Atlanta.

Barriers that kept blacks from voting came down in the 1960s, and schools were integrated. This meant that black children and white children began going to the same schools.

In 1964, Leroy Johnson became the first black Georgian of the 1900s to be elected to the Georgia senate. In 1972, Andrew Young of Georgia became the first black southerner in more than seventy years to be elected to the United States House of Representatives. And in 1973, Atlanta's Maynard Jackson became the first black person to be elected mayor of a big southern city. Jimmy Carter, a white Georgian who favored racial equality, also went far. In 1976, he was elected president of the United States. Carter was the first president to come from Georgia.

The growth of manufacturing has been one of the biggest changes in Georgia in recent years. Since 1950, many companies have been founded in Georgia. Many other firms moved there from other states. The growth in industry has drawn thousands of workers to Georgia. Between 1950 and 1990, Georgia's population nearly doubled, from 3.5 million to 6.5 million.

This growth has caused some problems. Pollution is one of those problems. By 1970, the

Jimmy Carter served as the thirty-ninth president from 1977 to 1981.

The midtown Atlanta skyline

Savannah River was filthy. Firms in Savannah and Augusta had dumped poisonous chemicals into the water. By the early 1990s, Georgians had partly cleaned the famous waterway. Atlanta has the state's worst air pollution. Recently, Atlanta's public transportation system has been expanded. Drivers have formed car pools. These measures should help clean up Atlanta's air.

Georgians are also working to improve their schools for both blacks and whites. In 1985, Georgia passed the Quality Basic Education Act (QBE). QBE has offered many new programs for students. Some are helping children do better in the early grades. Others are designed to keep older students in school. Georgians know that education is a key to making their state the kind of place Dr. King and James Oglethorpe dreamed it would be.

Georgians and Their Work

GEORGIANS AND THEIR WORK

As of 1990, Georgia was home to about 6.5 million people. Only ten other states had more people by that time. Georgia is a very fast-growing state. One day it may climb even higher on the population ladder.

Most Georgians are white. But the state has a very large black population. About one in every four Georgians is black. Georgia's Hispanic population is more than a hundred thousand. The state is also home to about thirteen thousand American Indians. Most of them are Creeks and Cherokees who have returned to Georgia.

Making and selling products is the main kind of work in Georgia. You may have used many Georgia products. Only one state—North Carolina—makes more textiles (cloth goods) than Georgia. Carpets, clothing, and yarn are three Georgia textiles you may have in your home. You may have traveled in one of the cars or airplanes that are made in the Atlanta area. Perhaps you have eaten peanut butter and drunk soda pop made in Georgia. The Empire State of the South may also have produced the paper you write on and the lumber for your home.

Only Mississippi, South Carolina, and Louisiana have a larger percentage of black people than Georgia.

Opposite: A young girl enjoying an Atlanta rain shower

Farming is still very important in Georgia. There are about fifty thousand farms in the state. Cotton is still grown, although in smaller amounts than in the mid-1800s. Georgia is a leader in growing peaches and in producing broiler chickens and eggs. Beef cattle, milk, hogs, watermelons, sweet potatoes, and tobacco are other Georgia farm goods. Georgia could claim to be the "nuttiest" state. For when it comes to growing peanuts and pecans, Georgia leads the nation.

Since Georgia is so famous for peanuts, it might be fun to see how many are grown there. About 2 billion pounds of peanuts are grown in Georgia every year. There are about two hundred peanut pods to a pound. There are usually two peanuts per pod. This makes a total of about 800 billion peanuts

Georgia is an important textile-making state.

grown in Georgia each year. End to end, all those peanuts would extend for 6 million miles—about twenty-five times the distance between the earth and the moon!

Georgia lies along the ocean, so fishing is important there, too. Shrimp and crabs are the main seafoods caught by Georgia fishermen. A lot of mining is also done. The state ranks first in mining clay and the very hard rock called granite.

Peanuts (left) and peaches (right) are two famous Georgia products. One Georgia county grows so many peaches that it was named Peach County.

Overleaf: A church on St. Simons Island

A Trip Through Georgia

A Trip Through Georgia

Georgia is a great state to visit. It has many kinds of scenery, from swamps to mountains. And few states have as many major historic sites. Atlanta is a good place to start a trip through Georgia. It is the state's capital and largest city.

Atlanta

Elephants at the Atlanta Zoo

Counting the suburbs, the Atlanta region is home to nearly half of all Georgians. Hartsfield International Airport, one of the world's busiest airports, helps make Atlanta a transportation center. Cable News Network (CNN), which is based there, helps make Atlanta a communications center. Atlanta is also a manufacturing city.

Atlanta is the most-wooded big city in America. Because of all its lovely dogwood trees, Atlanta is nicknamed the "Dogwood City."

The Georgia State Capitol has a golden dome. Some of that gold came from Dahlonega, the site of an early gold rush. Visitors can watch Georgia's state lawmakers at work inside the capitol.

Not far from the capitol, at 501 Auburn Avenue, is a very special house. Martin Luther King, Jr., was born and grew up in this house. Nearby is Ebenezer Baptist Church. Dr. King preached there with his father, who also was a minister. Next to the church is the grave of Dr. King, who was murdered at the age of only thirty-nine.

The Cyclorama, in Grant Park, is another highlight of Atlanta. It is one of the world's largest paintings. With its sound effects, the Cyclorama brings the Civil War Battle of Atlanta to life. The Atlanta Zoo is also in Grant Park.

There is a lot more to see and do in Atlanta. At the Woodruff Arts Center, visitors can see great

The Georgia State Capitol (left) and the Martin Luther King, Jr., gravesite (right)

35

Henry Aaron, baseball's all-time home-run leader, played for the Atlanta Braves.

The Coca-Cola Company has its world headquarters in Atlanta.

paintings or enjoy a play, an opera, or a symphony. Atlanta is also a big sports city. The Braves are Atlanta's major-league baseball team. The Falcons are its pro football team. The Hawks play pro basketball in the Georgia capital.

A walk down Peachtree Street can be fun. A seventy-three-story hotel on Peachtree is one of the world's tallest hotels. Peachtree Street has another claim to fame. In 1886, Coca-Cola was first sold in a drugstore on Peachtree Street.

Like most big cities, Atlanta has big problems. Nearly one-third of all Atlantans live in poverty. Crime and drugs plague the city. Atlantans will have to cooperate to solve these problems.

NORTHERN GEORGIA

Stone Mountain is a short way east of Atlanta. The world's largest sculpture has been carved into the side of Stone Mountain. It shows three Confederate heroes: President Jefferson Davis, General Robert E. Lee, and General Thomas "Stonewall" Jackson. The sculpture is so huge that thirty people once ate lunch on Lee's shoulder!

Northwest Georgia has two famous Civil War battlefields. Kennesaw Mountain Battlefield is not far from Stone Mountain. In Georgia's northwest corner is Chickamauga Battlefield, where the hillsides were said to have turned red with blood.

Near Kennesaw Mountain Battlefield are the Etowah Indian Mounds. Tools and pottery as much as a thousand years old have been found at these mounds. Nearby is New Echota, the early Cherokee capital. There, visitors can see how the Cherokee Indians lived before they were forced to walk the Trail of Tears.

The world's largest sculpture is carved into Stone Mountain.

Left: Panning for gold at Dahlonega
Right: A rushing stream in Amicalola Falls State Park

The Dahlonega Gold Museum is a good place to learn about the Georgia gold rush of the early 1800s. Nearby, visitors can pan for gold and keep what they find!

The mountains make northern Georgia one of the country's loveliest areas. In northeast Georgia, visitors can ride to the top of Brasstown Bald Mountain. From the top of the mountain, four states can be seen: Tennessee, North Carolina, South Carolina, and, of course, Georgia.

Many waterfalls add to the beauty of Georgia's northern highlands. Amicalola Falls plunges 729 feet over a ridge near Dawsonville. It is one of the prettiest sights in Georgia. The mountains are also a good place to spot deer, bears, foxes, and beavers.

One of the biggest cities in northeast Georgia, Athens, is near the mountains. Athens, named for the famous city of Athens, Greece, is home to the University of Georgia.

One University of Georgia graduate, Crawford Long, became the town doctor in Jefferson, Georgia, not far from Athens. Before Dr. Long's time, people had to stay awake during surgery. An operation was torture. In 1842, Long became the first doctor to use an anesthetic during surgery. The Crawford Long Museum is in Jefferson. The museum has displays that show how Dr. Long put people to sleep for operations.

The Federal Building and U.S. Courthouse in Macon

CENTRAL GEORGIA

Macon, Georgia's fourth-largest city, is southwest of Athens. Because it is close to the center of Georgia, Macon is called the "Heart of Georgia." People have lived in the Macon area for thousands of years. At Ocmulgee National Monument on the edge of Macon, tools and weapons made by prehistoric Indians can be seen. Mounds dating back about a thousand years can also be seen.

The Sidney Lanier cottage is another highlight of Macon. Lanier, a famous poet, was born in this house. Lake Sidney Lanier, on the Chattahoochee River, was named for him.

Before the Civil War, many rich cotton planters and merchants lived in and near Macon. Some of their homes look like palaces. Another side of Georgia's history can be seen at Macon's Harriet Tubman Historical and Cultural Museum. There, visitors can learn about black history and see artworks by Africans and African Americans.

Columbus, Georgia's second-biggest city, is southwest of Macon. The city lies along the

Children learn about black history at the Harriet Tubman Historical and Cultural Museum in Macon.

Chattahoochee River at the Alabama border. Columbus is a textile-making center. It was named for the great explorer, Christopher Columbus.

The Walker-Peters Langdon House is in Columbus. Built in 1828, it is thought to be the city's oldest home. A slightly older log cabin stands nearby, but it was not built in Columbus. It was moved from 10 miles away so that people could see how the early settlers lived. Fort Benning is just outside Columbus. It is an army base that is the main center for training U.S. paratroopers.

During the Civil War, a Confederate prison called Andersonville was southeast of Columbus. Captured Union troops were kept there. Up to thirty-three thousand men at a time were cramped into the prison. They didn't get the food or medicines they needed. In a short time, about thirteen thousand of them died. The scene of all this misery is now the Andersonville National Historic Site.

Plains, a Georgia town with a happier story, is a few miles southwest of Andersonville. The thirty-ninth president of the United States, Jimmy Carter, was born in Plains. Carter's childhood home, school, and other buildings important in his life can be seen in and near Plains. Jimmy Carter himself can often be seen in Plains.

This monument at the Andersonville National Historic Site shows Iowa, in the form of a woman, weeping for the sons she lost.

Alligators, which live in Okefenokee Swamp, can stay under warm water without coming up for about fifteen minutes. They can stay under cold water for more than an hour.

Manatees, which can sometimes be seen around Cumberland Island, are also known as sea cows.

SOUTHERN GEORGIA AND THE COAST

Albany is on the Flint River not far from Georgia's southwest corner. It is Georgia's fifth-largest city. Albany has a zoo called the Chehaw Wild Animal Park. Astronauts Monument is also in Albany. It honors America's space explorers who died in the *Challenger* explosion of 1986.

There are no big cities in far southern Georgia except for Albany. There are plenty of farms in the region, though. Farmers in southern Georgia grow plenty of peanuts, pecans, cotton, and corn. They also raise large numbers of beef cattle, hogs, and chickens.

Near Georgia's southeast corner, along the Florida border, is a huge wetland. This is Georgia's famous Okefenokee Swamp. Visitors can take boat tours of the swamp. Most of the swamp is a wildlife refuge. No hunting is allowed there. Bears, deer, and birds such as egrets live in the swamp. Alligators live there, too, some of them up to 15 feet long.

The Atlantic Ocean is about 50 miles east of Okefenokee Swamp. Georgia's 100-mile coast is very different from its inland mountains and farms. Fishing boats and beautiful views of the ocean can be seen. Off the coast are the Golden Isles and

other islands. Many of them can be reached by bridge or ferryboat. The Golden Isles are great places for lovers of wildlife. Loggerhead turtles weighing up to 600 pounds can be seen. A 1,500-pound sea animal called the manatee can sometimes be seen around Cumberland Island. The marshes of the Golden Isles are also home to alligators.

Two famous old forts can be visited on Georgia's islands. Fort Frederica, on St. Simons Island, stands not far from where the Battle of Bloody Marsh was fought. Fort Pulaski was completed in 1847 on Cockspur Island, not far from Savannah. Scars from cannon fire can be seen on its

Fort Pulaski National Monument is on Cockspur Island near Savannah. Completed in 1847, the fort was used in the Civil War.

walls. They were made when Union forces captured Fort Pulaski in 1862.

SAVANNAH AND AUGUSTA

Savannah, Georgia's third-largest city, lies along the Savannah River near the coast. Savannah is one of America's prettiest cities. More than twenty public squares—with their flowers and trees—help make it beautiful. The squares were the idea of Georgia's founder, James Oglethorpe.

Savannah is called the "Mother City of Georgia" because it was the colony's first European town. A plaque marks the spot where James Oglethorpe landed with the first settlers in 1733. More than a thousand buildings dating back a hundred years or more still stand in Savannah.

A house at 142 Bull Street is a highlight of Savannah. Juliette Low, who founded the Girl Scouts of America, was born in this house. Inside are several artworks that Juliette Low created.

Many places relating to black history can also be seen in Savannah. In 1775, the first black church congregation in North America was founded in Savannah. It was called the First African Baptist Church. The present church, built in 1859, can be

The Telfair Academy of Arts and Sciences in Savannah is the oldest art museum in the South. It is housed in a mansion built in the early 1800s.

visited on Montgomery Street. Runaway slaves hid under the floorboards of this church before the Civil War.

Augusta, 100 miles up the Savannah River from Savannah, is a good place to end a trip through Georgia. Augusta has long been a center for buying and selling cotton and for making cotton goods. Augusta's Cotton Exchange Building dates from 1886. A museum in the building shows what cotton has meant to the South over the years.

Augusta also hosts Georgia's most-famous yearly event. It is called the Masters Golf Tournament. The Masters was founded in 1934 by Bobby Jones, a great golfer who was born in Atlanta.

Left: Live oak trees shade the lawns of many historic Savannah mansions. Right: Augusta's Cotton Exchange Building

A Gallery of Famous Georgians

A GALLERY OF FAMOUS GEORGIANS

Georgia has been home to many famous people. One reason for this is that Georgia is one of our oldest states.

James Oglethorpe (1696-1785) was born in London, England. At fourteen, he joined the English army. Later, he won a seat in the English government. When Oglethorpe was in his early thirties, a friend of his died in debtors' prison. This helped plant the idea in Oglethorpe's mind for a debtors' colony. The "Father of Georgia" spent more than six years in Georgia. He died in England at nearly ninety years of age.

Button Gwinnett (1735?-1777) was born in England. His strange first name was a last name from his mother's side of the family. When he was about thirty, Gwinnett moved to America. He became a leading Georgia patriot. He signed the Declaration of Independence. He also served briefly as Georgia's governor. Gwinnett died in a gun duel less than a year after signing the Declaration of Independence.

Alexander H. Stephens (1812-1883) was born in what is now Taliaferro County, Georgia. He

This statue of James Oglethorpe stands in Savannah's Chippewa Square.

Opposite: President Jimmy Carter and his wife Rosalynn bicycling with members of the family

Alexander Stephens was called "Little Aleck" because he never weighed more than one hundred pounds.

W. E. B. Du Bois was a famous black American author who taught at Atlanta University.

taught school for a while. Later, he became a Georgia lawmaker. Stephens tried his best to prevent the Civil War. Yet when the southern states broke away, he served as the Confederate vice-president. After the war, he was imprisoned for six months. Stephens was elected governor of Georgia in 1883. He died after serving just a few months.

Juliette Low (1860-1927) was born in Savannah on Halloween. In 1909, a group called the Girl Guides was begun in England. Low felt that American girls would like to belong to such a group. In the spring of 1912, she formed the first United States Girl Guides troop in Savannah. She soon changed the name to the Girl Scouts. Low died in Savannah at the age of sixty-six.

Georgia has been home to many fine authors. The great writer **W. E. B. Du Bois** (1868-1963) was born in Massachusetts. In 1895, he became the first black person to earn a doctoral degree at Harvard University. Later, Dr. Du Bois taught at Atlanta University. He wrote a famous book of essays, *The Souls of Black Folk*. In the 1920s, Dr. Du Bois edited a magazine for black children. It was called *The Brownies' Book*.

Author **Margaret Mitchell** (1900-1949) was born in Atlanta. She wrote a very famous novel about the Civil War period. Called *Gone With the Wind*, it is one of the most popular novels of all time. It was made into a famous movie that won the Academy Award for the best film of 1939.

Carson McCullers (1917-1967) was born in Columbus. She had a special gift for writing about human feelings. Her novels include *The Heart Is a Lonely Hunter* and *The Member of the Wedding*.

Georgia has also produced many great athletes. **Ty Cobb** (1886-1961) was born in Banks County, Georgia. Cobb was one of the best players in baseball history. His .367 lifetime average and 2,245 runs scored are major-league records.

Juliette Low (left) founded the Girl Scouts in Savannah. The Girl Scouts celebrate Founders Day on her birthday, October 31.

Jackie Robinson, who joined the Brooklyn Dodgers in 1947, was the first black major-league baseball player.

Jackie Robinson (1919-1972) was born in Cairo, Georgia. When Robinson was growing up, black people weren't allowed to play major-league baseball. In 1947, Robinson joined the Brooklyn Dodgers. He was the first black major leaguer. Over ten seasons, he batted .311. In 1949, he won the National League batting title and Most Valuable Player award.

Jim Brown was born on St. Simons Island in 1936. He became a great football star. Playing fullback, Brown ran for 12,312 yards in his nine years with the Cleveland Browns. Many people call him the greatest running back in football history.

Oliver Hardy (1892-1957) was born in Harlem, Georgia. When he was about eighteen, Hardy opened the first movie theater in Milledgeville, Georgia. He felt that he could make funnier films than those his theater showed. He became a movie actor and got his chance to prove it. He did not have much success until he teamed up with Stan Laurel in 1926. Laurel and Hardy became a famous comedy team. They made more than a hundred Laurel and Hardy films.

Jimmy Carter was born James Earl Carter, Jr., in Plains, Georgia, in 1924. As a child, Jimmy made a dollar a day selling peanuts on the streets of Plains.

Oliver Hardy (right), shown here with his partner, Stan Laurel, once said that he based his movie character on the "Helpful Henry" cartoon that appeared in Georgia newspapers when he was a boy.

He served on battleships and submarines in the U.S. Navy. Then he returned to run the family peanut business in Plains. Carter entered politics in 1962. Within a few years, he was elected governor of Georgia. Later, as president, Carter was known as a man of peace and a leader who cared about people.

Martin Luther King, Jr., (1929-1968) was born in Atlanta. He was only fifteen when he entered Morehouse College. Dr. King became a famous minister and civil-rights leader. He led marches and gave speeches about civil rights for black people. He also wrote books. Dr. King kept up his work even after his house was bombed and he was stabbed. In 1963, Dr. King gave his "I have a Dream" speech in Washington, D.C. It is one of the most famous speeches in United States history. The next year he won the Nobel Peace Prize for his work. Sadly, Dr. King was shot and killed in 1968.

Andrew Young was born in 1932 in New Orleans, Louisiana. He became a minister, serving

Dr. Martin Luther King, Jr., (front right) leading a civil-rights march

churches in Georgia and Alabama. Georgians elected Young to the U.S. Congress in 1972. Five years later, he became the first black U.S. ambassador to the United Nations (UN). Young served as the mayor of Atlanta from 1981 to 1989.

Jessye Norman was born in Augusta in 1945. She studied music at Howard University and then became an opera singer. By the 1980s, she was one of the world's most famous opera stars.

Newt Gingrich was born in Harrisburg, Pennsylvania in 1943. He was educated in Georgia. Gingrich was elected to Congress as a Republican in 1979. He became the Speaker of the U.S. House of Representatives in 1995.

President Jimmy Carter chose Andrew Young as the U.S. ambassador to the UN.

Home to Tomochichi, James Oglethorpe, Dr. Martin Luther King, Jr., President Jimmy Carter, and Juliette Low...

The place where the cotton gin was invented, where anesthesia was first used in an operation, and where the Girl Scouts of America began . . .

A land where there is a huge rock eagle and real live alligators . . .

A state that is a leader in growing peanuts and making textiles . . .

That is Georgia—the Empire State of the South!

Did You Know?

From 1838 to 1861, the United States minted gold coins at Dahlonega, Georgia. They were marked with a *D* and today are very valuable.

Georgia's Rebecca Latimer Felton was the first woman United States senator. She replaced a senator who had died, and served only two days in 1922.

There is a town named Santa Claus, Georgia.

In 1970, circus performer Karl Wallenda walked across a 1,000-foot-long tightrope stretched 750 feet above Tallulah Gorge, in northeast Georgia. Wallenda was sixty-five years old at the time.

Actress Tallulah Bankhead was named for her grandmother, who had been named for Tallulah Falls, in northeast Georgia.

The Braves, a National League baseball team, moved to Atlanta from Milwaukee in 1966.

Martin Luther King, Jr., entered Atlanta's Booker T. Washington High School when he was thirteen. King skipped two years and finished high school at fifteen.

Ty Cobb, known as the "Georgia Peach," won twelve batting titles, including nine in a row. He was a member of a well-known Georgia family. One relative, Howell Cobb, was governor of Georgia from 1851 to 1853. Cobb County was named for another relative, Senator Thomas Cobb.

Georgia has counties named Bacon, Coffee, and Peach.

Former president Jimmy Carter sometimes mows the lawn and teaches Sunday School at his church in Plains.

In 1990, Atlanta was picked to host the 1996 Summer Olympics.

Ray Charles, the famous pianist and singer who became blind as a child, was born in Albany. One of his best-loved recordings is "Georgia on My Mind."

Every December, a college football game called the Peach Bowl is played in Atlanta.

The word *goober* is thought to come from *nguba,* an African word for *peanut.*

Kenesaw Mountain Landis was the first baseball commissioner. He was named for Georgia's Kennesaw Mountain, where his father had been wounded in the Civil War. But his father spelled the name with only one *n* instead of two.

55

GEORGIA INFORMATION

Area: 58,910 square miles (twenty-first among the states in size)

Greatest Distance North to South: 318 miles

Greatest Distance East to West: 278 miles

Coastline: 100 miles

Borders: Tennessee and North Carolina to the north; South Carolina and the Atlantic Ocean to the east; Florida to the south; Florida and Alabama to the west

Highest Point: Brasstown Bald Mountain, 4,784 feet above sea level

Lowest Point: Sea level, along the Atlantic Ocean

Hottest Recorded Temperature: 113° F. (at Greenville, on May 27, 1978)

Coldest Recorded Temperature: -17° F. (in Floyd County, northwest Georgia, on January 27, 1940)

Statehood: The fourth state, on January 2, 1788

Origin of Name: Georgia was named for England's King George II

Capital: Atlanta

Previous Capitals: Savannah, Augusta, Louisville, and Milledgeville

Counties: 159

United States Senators: 2

United States Representatives: 11 (as of 1992)

State Senators: 56

State Representatives: 180

State Song: "Georgia on My Mind," by Stuart Gorrell (words) and Hoagy Carmichael (melody)

State Motto: "Wisdom, Justice, and Moderation"

Cherokee rose

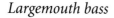

Largemouth bass

Nicknames: "Empire State of the South," "Peach State," "Goober State"

State Seal: Adopted in 1914

State Flag: Adopted in 1956

State Flower: Cherokee rose

State Bird: Brown thrasher

State Tree: Live oak

State Fish: Largemouth bass

State Insect: Honeybee

State Butterfly: Tiger swallowtail

State Wildflower: Azalea

State Game Bird: Bobwhite quail

State Fossil: Shark tooth

State Gem: Quartz

State Mineral: Staurolite crystals

Some Rivers: Savannah, Ogeechee, Oconee, Ocmulgee, Altamaha, Flint, Chattahoochee

Some Islands: Blackbeard, Cumberland, Jekyll, St. Catherines, St. Simons, Sea, Tybee

Wildlife: Bears, deer, alligators, foxes, beavers, opossums, raccoons, rabbits, sea turtles and other kinds of turtles, rattlesnakes and other snakes, egrets, ducks, brown thrashers, and many other kinds of birds

Fishing Products: Shrimps, crabs, oysters, clams, red snappers, shad

Farm Products: Peanuts, pecans, peaches, broiler chickens, eggs, beef cattle, milk, hogs, watermelons, sweet potatoes, tobacco, cotton, soybeans, corn

Mining: Clay, granite, marble, limestone, sand and gravel

Manufactured Products: Carpeting and other textiles, airplanes, cars, peanut butter and other foods, soft drinks, paper, lumber, various wood products, chemicals

Population: 6,478,216, eleventh among the states (1990 U.S. Census Bureau figures)

Major Cities (1990 Census):

Atlanta	394,017	Albany	78,122
Columbus	178,681	Roswell	47,923
Savannah	137,560	Athens	45,734
Macon	106,612	Augusta	44,639

Honeybee

Live oak trees

GEORGIA HISTORY

This man in a Confederate uniform took part in a Civil War reenactment in Rome, Georgia.

1540—Hernando De Soto of Spain travels through Georgia

1566—The Spanish build a fort on Georgia's St. Catherines Island

1690—The Spanish abandon Georgia by about this time

1732—England's King George II grants a charter to create the colony of Georgia

1733—James Oglethorpe leads the first English settlers to Georgia

1742—The English beat the Spanish in the Battle of Bloody Marsh

1754—Georgia becomes a royal colony

1763—The colony's first newspaper, the *Georgia Gazette,* is founded in Savannah

1775—The Revolutionary War against England begins

1778—The English capture Savannah

1782—English troops are finally driven out of Georgia

1783—The Revolutionary War ends with an American victory

1788—Georgia becomes the fourth state

1793—Eli Whitney invents the cotton gin in Georgia

1800—Georgia's population is about 163,000

1827—Gold is discovered in northern Georgia; by this year, the Creeks have been forced out of Georgia

1828—The *Cherokee Phoenix,* the first Indian newspaper in the country, is printed at New Echota

1837—The town of Terminus (now Atlanta) is founded

1838—The Cherokees are forced out of Georgia

1861—Georgia withdraws from the Union and joins the Confederacy; the Civil War begins on April 12

1863—About 34,000 men are killed or wounded as the Confederates win the Battle of Chickamauga Creek

1864—The Confederates win the Battle of Kennesaw Mountain on June 27; later in the year, Union General William Tecumseh Sherman burns Atlanta and marches to the sea

1865—The Union defeats the Confederacy; the Civil War ends

1868—Atlanta becomes Georgia's capital

1870—Georgia once again becomes part of the United States

1900—Georgia's population reaches about 2.2 million

1912—Juliette Low founds the Girl Scouts of America at Savannah

1917-18—About 95,000 Georgians help the United States and its allies win World War I

1920s—Boll weevils destroy much of Georgia's cotton crop

1929-39—During the Great Depression, many Georgia factories close

1941-45—About 320,000 Georgians help the United States and its allies win World War II

1943—Georgia becomes the first state to permit eighteen-year-olds to vote

1964—Dr. Martin Luther King, Jr., receives the Nobel Peace Prize; Leroy Johnson becomes the first black Georgian of the century to win election to the state senate

1972—Andrew Young of Georgia becomes the first black southerner elected to the U.S. House of Representatives in more than seventy years

1973—Atlanta's Maynard Jackson becomes the first black person elected mayor of a big southern city

1976—Jimmy Carter, of Plains, is elected president

1983—Georgia's current state constitution goes into effect; Georgia celebrates the 250th anniversary of its founding as a colony

1986—Georgia's Quality Basic Education Act (QBE) goes into effect

1988—Happy 200th Birthday, Empire State of the South!

1990—Georgia's population reaches about 6.5 million

1994—Tropical storm Alberto hits the west central and southwest areas of the state, causing disastrous floods and displacing more than 8,000 families

In 1964, Leroy R. Johnson became the first black Georgian of the century to win election to the state senate.

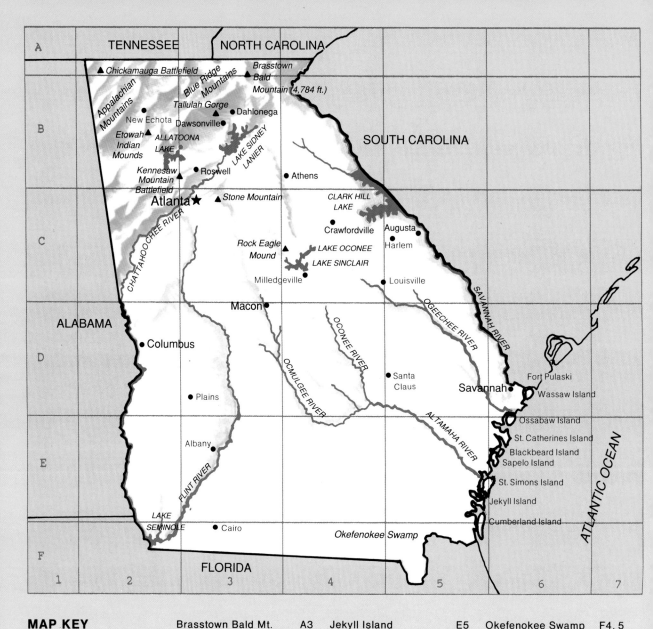

TENNESSEE   NORTH CAROLINA

▲ Chickamauga Battlefield

*Brasstown
Bald
Mountain (4,784 ft.)*

Blue Ridge Mountains

Appalachian Mountains

Tallulah Gorge

• New Echota
Dawsonville
• Dahlonega

▲ New Echota

Etowah Indian Mounds ▲

ALLATOONA LAKE

SOUTH CAROLINA

LAKE SIDNEY LANIER

Kennesaw Mountain Battlefield ▲

• Roswell

• Athens

Atlanta ★   ▲ *Stone Mountain*

CLARK HILL LAKE

• Crawfordville   • Augusta
Harlem

Rock Eagle Mound ▲

LAKE OCONEE

LAKE SINCLAIR

• Milledgeville

• Louisville

ALABAMA

CHATTAHOOCHEE RIVER

Macon •

OCONEE RIVER

OGEECHEE RIVER

SAVANNAH RIVER

• Columbus

OCMULGEE RIVER

• Santa Claus

Fort Pulaski

Savannah •   Wassaw Island

• Plains

ALTAMAHA RIVER

Ossabaw Island

St. Catherines Island

Blackbeard Island
Sapelo Island

Albany •

FLINT RIVER

St. Simons Island

Jekyll Island

ATLANTIC OCEAN

LAKE SEMINOLE   • Cairo

Cumberland Island

Okefenokee Swamp

FLORIDA

1   2   3   4   5   6   7

MAP KEY

Brasstown Bald Mt.	A3
Cairo	F3
Chattahoochee River	C2
Chickamauga Battlefield	A2
Clark Hill Lake	C4
Columbus	D2
Crawfordville	C4
Cumberland Island	E, F5
Dahlonega	B3
Dawsonville	B3
Etowah Indian Mounds	B2
Flint River	E3
Fort Pulaski	D6
Harlem	C5

Albany E3
Allatoona Lake B2
Altamaha River E5
Appalachian Mountains B2
Athens B4
Atlanta C3
Augusta C5
Blackbeard Island E6
Blue Ridge Mountains B3

Jekyll Island E5
Kennesaw Mountain
   Battlefield B2, 3
Lake Sinclair C4
Lake Seminole F2
Lake Sidney Lanier B3
Lake Oconee C4
Louisville C4, 5
Macon D3
Milledgeville C4
New Echota B2
Ocmulgee River D4
Oconee River D4
Ogeechee River D5

Okefenokee Swamp F4, 5
Ossabaw Island E5
Plains D3
Rock Eagle Mound C4
Roswell B3
Santa Claus D5
Sapelo Island E6
Savannah River B4, C5, D6
Savannah D6
St. Catherines Island E6
St. Simons Island E5, 6
Stone Mountain C3
Tallulah Gorge B3
Wassaw Island D6

GLOSSARY

ambassador: A person who represents, or acts as an agent for, a country

anesthetic: A medicine that puts people to sleep for surgery

ban: To forbid by law

bluff: A high, steep bank with a flat or rounded front; a cliff

capital: The city that is the seat of government

capitol: The building in which the government meets

civil rights: The rights of a citizen

climate: The weather of a region

colonize: To found a colony

debtors: People who owe money

doctoral degree: The highest degree that is given by a university; a doctorate

duel: A formal fight in the presence of witnesses between two persons who use deadly weapons

equality: The state of being equal

essays: Short pieces of writing on a subject

expanded: Enlarged

explorers: Those who travel in unknown lands to seek information

imprisoned: Kept in prison

inland: Away from the shore; toward the interior

issued: Put out to the public; published

key: Of major importance

missions: Places where religious work is carried on; churches

novel: A book of fiction; a story

officially: Authorized, or legally approved, by the government

pan for gold: Wash earth or gravel in a pan to look for gold

paratroopers: Soldiers who parachute, or jump from aircraft, into a combat zone

patriot: A person who loves and supports his country

plague: Do evil; afflict; harm; damage

plantations: Huge farms

plaque: A flat piece of metal with written information on it

plunges: Moves downward rapidly

poverty: The state of being poor

prehistoric: Before written history

racial justice: Fair treatment of people of all races

sculpture: Artwork that has been made by carving, chiseling, or molding hard materials

squares: Open spaces in a city that are often used as parks

suburbs: Towns or villages that developed near large cities

trustees: People who were entrusted to supervise a colony

wrecked: Ruined; destroyed; damaged

PICTURE ACKNOWLEDGMENTS

Front cover: © **SuperStock**; 1, © Claude Haycraft/**Tony Stone Worldwide/Chicago Ltd.**; 2, **Tom Dunnington**; 3, **Georgia Department of Industry, Trade & Tourism**; 5, **Tom Dunnington**; 6-7, © **Gene Ahrens**; 8, © W. Metzen/**H. Armstrong Roberts**; 9 (left), **Courtesy of Hammond, Incorporated, Maplewood, New Jersey**; 9 (right), © Ken Dequaine Photography/**Third Coast Stock Source**; 10, © **Gene Ahrens**; 11 (left), © Fred Whitehead/**Nawrocki Stock Photo**; 11 (middle), © Edna Douthat/**Root Resources**; 11 (right), © Jerry Hennen; 12-13, **Atlanta Historical Society**; 14, © **Richard & Mary Magruder**; 15, **Historical Pictures Service, Chicago**; 16 (left), **North Wind Picture Archives**; 16 (right), **Historical Pictures Service, Chicago**; 17, **Hargrett Rare Book Library, University of Georgia**; 18, **North Wind Picture Archives**; 19, **Georgia Department of Industry, Trade & Tourism**; 20 (left), **Historical Pictures Service, Chicago**; 20 (right), **Photri**; 22 (both pictures), **Historical Pictures Service, Chicago**; 23, **Historical Pictures Service, Chicago**; 25, **AP/Wide World Photos**; 27, © **Dot Griffith**; 28, © **Lynne Siler**; 30, © **SuperStock**; 31 (left), © Bill Barksdale/**Root Resources**; 31 (right), © Charles McNulty/**Tony Stone Worldwide/Chicago Ltd.**; 32-33, © G. Ahrens/**H. Armstrong Roberts**; 34, © **David J. Forbert Photography**; 35 (left), © **Gene Ahrens**; 35 (right), © **David J. Forbert Photography**; 36 (top), **AP/Wide World Photos**; 36 (bottom), © **Dot Griffith**; 37, © **SuperStock**; 38 (left), © **William Schemmel Photo**; 38 (right), © **Lynn M. Stone**; 39, © **David J. Forbert Photography**; 40, © **David J. Forbert Photography**; 41, **Georgia Department of Industry, Trade & Tourism**; 42 (top), © Jerry Hennen; 42 (bottom), © **Joan Dunlop**; 43, © **Joan Dunlop**; 44, © **David J. Forbert Photography**; 45 (left), © **Gene Ahrens**; 45 (right), **Augusta/Richmond County Convention & Visitors Bureau**; 46, **Courtesy: Jimmy Carter Library**; 47, © **William Schemmel**; 48 (top), **Historical Pictures Service, Chicago**; 48 (bottom), **AP/Wide World Photos**; 49 (left), **AP/Wide World Photos**; 49 (right), © **Courtesy, Girl Scouts of the USA**; 50, **AP/Wide World Photos**; 51, **AP/Wide World Photos**; 52, **AP/Wide World Photos**; 53, **AP/Wide World Photos**; 54 (bottom left), © **Joan Dunlop**; 54 (top right), **AP/Wide World Photos**; 55 (bottom left), **Photri**; 55 (top right), © Max & Bea Hunn/**Journalism Services**; 56 (top), **Courtesy Flag Research Center, Winchester, Massachusetts 01890**; 56 (middle), © Mary A. Root/**Root Resources**; 56 (bottom), © **Jerry Hennen**; 57 (top), © D. Muench/**H. Armstrong Roberts**; 57 (bottom), © Gene Ahrens/**SuperStock**; 58, **Georgia Department of Industry, Trade & Tourism**; 59, **AP/Wide World Photos**; 60, Tom Dunnington; back cover, © Ken Dequaine Photography/**Third Coast Stock Source**

INDEX

Page numbers in boldface type indicate illustrations.

Aaron, Henry, **36**
Alabama, 8
Albany, 42
alphabet, Cherokee, **22**
Altamaha River, 11
Amicalola Falls, 38-39
Andersonville National Historic
  Site, 41, **41**
anesthesia, first use of, 39, 53
animals, 14, 39, 42, **42**, 43, 53, 56, 57
Anna Ruby Falls, 9
Anne (ship), 16
Appalachian Mountains, 9
Athens, 39
Atlanta, **front cover**, 10, 21, 24, **27**,
  29, 34-36, **34**, **35**, **36**, 55
Atlanta, Battle of, 35
Atlanta Braves, 4, 36, **36**, 54
Atlanta Falcons, 36
Atlanta Hawks, 4, 36
Atlanta Zoo, **34**
Atlantic Ocean, 4, 8, 42
Augusta, 17, 19, 24, 27, 45, **45**
Bacon County, 55
Baldwin, Abraham, 20
Bankhead, Tallulah, 54
black people (African Americans),
  18, 21, 23, 25-26, 29, 40, **40**, 44-45,
  48, **48**, 50, **50**, 51-53, **52**, **53**, **59**
Bloody Marsh, Battle of, 17-18, 43
Blue Ridge Mountains, 4, 9
bluegrass musicians, 3
boll weevils, 24
bordering states, 8, 56
Brasstown Bald Mountain, 9, 38
Brown, Jim, 50
Carter Jimmy, 4, 26, 41, **46**, 50-51, 53,
  55
Charles, Ray, 55
Chattahoochee River, 11, 40, 41
Cherokee Indians, 14, 22, **22**, 29, 37
Cherokee Phoenix, 22
Chickamauga Battlefield, 37
Chickamauga Creek, Battle of, 23, **23**
Chippewa Square, **47**

civil rights, 25-26, 51-52
Civil War, 23-24, 35, 36-37, 40, 41,
  43-44, 48
climate, 4, 17, 56
Cobb, Howell, 55
Cobb, Thomas, 54
Cobb, Ty, 49, 54, **54**
Cobb County, 54
Coca-Cola Company, 36, **36**
Cockspur Island, 43, **43**
Coffee County, 55
colonial times, 15-19
Columbus, 10, 21, 40-41
Columbus, Christopher, 41
Confederate States of America,
  23-24, **23**, 36, 48, **58**
Congress, U.S., 26, 53
Constitution, U.S., 19-20
Cotton Day, **12-13**
cotton, 20-21, 24, 30, 40, 42, 45
Cotton Exchange buildings, 45, **45**
cotton gin, 20, **20**, 53
Creek Indians, 14, 21, 29
Creek War, 21
Cumberland Island, 9, 42, 43
Dahlonega, 34, 38, **38**, 54
Darien, 17
Davis, Jefferson, 36
Dawsonville, 38
debtors' colony, 15-16, 47
Declaration of Independence, 19, 47
De Soto, Hernando, 15, **15**
Du Bois, W. E. B., 48, **48**
Ebenezer, 17
Ebenezer Baptist Church, 35
education, 22, 25, 26, 27, 39
England, 15-16, 17-19
Etowah Indian Mounds, **14**, 37
explorers, Spanish, 15, **15**
farming, 4, 18, 20-21, 24, 25, 30-31,
  31, 40, 42, 45, 57
"Father of Georgia," 47
Felton, Rebecca Latimer, 54
Few, William, 19-20
fishing, 31, **56**, 57

flag of Georgia, **56**, 57
Flint River, 11, 42
Florida, 8, 15, 16, 42
flowers, 4, 44, **56**
Flowery Branch, **12-13**
Fort Benning, 41
Fort Frederica, **19**, 43
Fort Pulaski, 43-44, **43**
geography of Georgia, 8-9, 56, 57
George II, King, 16
Gingrich, Newt, 53
Girl Scouts of America, 44, 48, **49**, 53
gold, 15, 22, 34, 38, 54
Golden Isles, 4, 8-9, 42-43
"goobers," 4, 55
government of Georgia, 16, 18, 22, 24,
  34
Guale, 15, 16
Gwinnett, Button, 19, 47
Hall, Lyman, 19
Hardy, Oliver, 50, **51**
Hispanic people, 29
history of Georgia, 14-27, 36-37, 38,
  39, 40, 41, 43-45, 58-59
House of Representatives, U.S., 26
Indians, 14, 17, **17**, 19, 21-22, **22**, 29,
  37, **39**
industry, 4, 25, 26, 29, **30**, 41, 57
integration, 25, 26
islands, 1, 8-9, **8**, 15, 17, **32-33**,
  42-43, **43**, 57
Jackson, Maynard, 26
Jackson, Thomas "Stonewall," 36
Jefferson, 39
Jekyll Island, 9
Jewish people, 17
Johnson, Leroy, 26, **59**
Jones, Bobby, 45
Kennesaw Mountain, Battle of, 23, 55
Kennesaw Mountain Battlefield,
  36-37
King, Martin Luther, Jr., 4, 25, **25**,
  27, 35, 51-52, **52**, 53, 54

Ku Klux Klan (KKK), 25
Landis, Kenesaw Mountain, **55**
Lanier, Sidney, 40
Laurel, Stan, 50, **51**
Lee, Robert E., 36
Long, Crawford, 39
Louisiana, 29
Louisville, 24
Low, Juliette, 44, 48, **49**, 53
Macon, 10, 21, 39-40, **39**, **40**
manufacturing, 25, 26, 29, **30**, 34,
   40, 57
maps of Georgia showing:
   cities and geographical features, **60**
   early settlement, **18**
   location in U.S., **2**
   products and history, **5**
   topography, **9**
Marthasville (Atlanta), 21
McCullers, Carson, 49
Milledgeville, 24
mining, 31, 57
Mississippi, 29
Mississippi River, 8
Mitchell, Margaret, 48-49
mounds, Indian, 14, **14**, 37, 39
mountains, 4, 9-10, 36-37, **37**, 38-39
museums, 38, 39, 40, **40**, 44, **44**
New Echota, 22, 37
nicknames, Georgia's, 4, 57
Norman, Jessye, 53
North Carolina, 8, 29, 38
Nunes, Samuel, 17
Ocmulgee National Monument, 39
Ocmulgee River, 11
Oconee River, 11
Ogeechee River, 11
Oglethorpe, James, 15-18, **16**, 27,
   44, 47, **47**, 53
Okefenokee Swamp, **10**, 11, 42

Oklahoma, 21, 22
Olympics of 1996, 55
Ossabaw Island, 8
Peach Bowl, 55
Peach County, 31, 55
peaches, 4, 24, 30, **31**
peanuts, 4, 24, 30-31, **31**, 42, 53, 55
people of Georgia, 25, 29, 47-53
Piedmont, the, 10
Plains, 41, 55
plants, 4, 11, **11**, 34, **45**, 56, 57
pollution, 26-27
population, 25, 26, 29, 57
prehistoric Georgia, 14, 37, 39
products of Georgia, 4, **5**, 29-31, **30**,
   31, 42, 53, 57
Providence Canyon State Park, 6-7,
   back cover
public transportation, 27
Quality Basic Education Act (QBE),
   27
Revolutionary War, 18-19
rivers, 11, 27, 57
Robinson, Jackie, 50, **50**
Rock Eagle Mound, 14
St. Catherines Island, 8-9, 15
St. Simons Island, **1**, **8**, 9, 17, **32-33**,
   43
Salzburgers, 17
Santa Claus, 54
Sapelo Island, 9
Savannah, 17, 19, 24, 27, 43, 44-45,
   44, **45**
Savannah River, 11, 16, 26-27, 44, 45
schools, 22, 25, 26, 27, 39
Sea Island, 9
Senate, U.S., 54
Sequoya, 22, **22**
settlers, 14-18, **16**, 21, 41
Sherman, William Tecumseh, 24

Sidney Lanier, Lake, 40
size of Georgia, 8, 56
slavery, 16, 18, 21, 23, 24, 45
South Carolina, 8, 16, 29, 38
Spain and Spaniards, 15, 17
sports, 4, 36, **36**, 45, 49, 50, **50**, 54,
   54, 55
state parks, **6-7**, **9**, **38**
state symbols, 57
statehood, 20, 56
Stephens, Alexander H., 47-48, **48**
Stone Mountain, 36-37, **37**
swamps, 10-11, **10**, 42, 43
Tallulah Gorge, 54
taxes on colonies, 18
Telfair Academy of Arts and
   Sciences, 44, **44**
Tennessee, 8, 38
Terminus (Atlanta), 21
textile industry, 29, **30**, 41
Tomochichi, 17, **17**, 53
topography of Georgia, 9-11, 56, 57
Trail of Tears, 22, 37
trees, 4, 11, **11**, 34, 44, **45**, 57
Unicoi State Park, **9**
United Nations, 53
University of Georgia, 39
Virginia, 19
voting rights, 25, 26
Wallenda, Karl, 54
Walton, George, 19
War of Jenkins' Ear, 17
Wassaw Island, 8
waterfalls, **9**, 38-39
Wayne, "Mad" Anthony, 19
Whitney, Eli, 20, **20**
Yamacraw Bluff, 16-17, **16**
Yamacraw Indians, 17
Yorktown, Battle of, 19
Young, Andrew, 26, 52-53, **53**

ABOUT THE AUTHOR

Dennis Fradin attended Northwestern University on a partial creative scholarship and graduated in 1967. He has published stories and articles in such places as *Ingenue, The Saturday Evening Post, Scholastic, Chicago, Oui,* and *National Humane Review.* His previous books include the Thirteen Colonies series and the Young People's Stories of Our States series for Childrens Press, and *Bad Luck Tony* for Prentice-Hall. In the True Book series, Dennis has written about astronomy, farming, comets, archaeology, movies, space colonies, the space lab, explorers, and pioneers. He is married and the father of three children.